W9-BRV-610

Texts for Fluency Practice

Level A

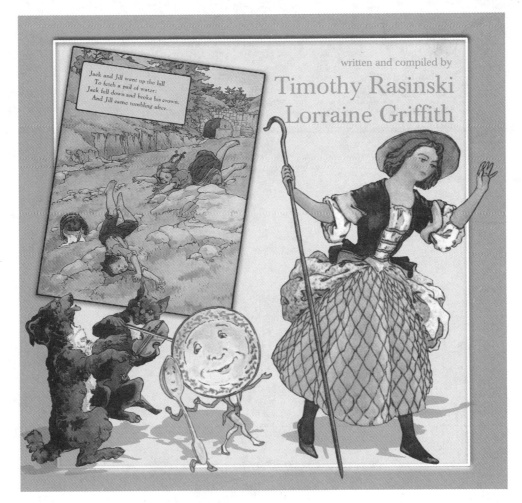

written and compiled by
Timothy Rasinski
Lorraine Griffith

Jack and Jill went up the hill
To fetch a pail of water.
Jack fell down and broke his crown,
And Jill came tumbling after.

Authors

Timothy Rasinski and Lorraine Griffith

Editor
Tracy Edmunds

Imaging
Alfred Lau

Product Director
Phil Garcia

Cover Design
Lee Aucoin

Creative Director
Lee Aucoin

Editor-in-Chief
Sharon Coan, M.S. Ed.

Publisher
Corinne Burton, M.S. Ed.

Shell Education

5301 Oceanus Drive

Huntington Beach, CA 92649-1030

www.shelleducation.com

ISBN 978-1-4258-0398-8

©2005 Shell Education

Made in U.S.A.

Reprinted, 2007

The classroom teacher may reproduce copies of materials in this book for classroom use only. The reproduction of any part for an entire school or school system is strictly prohibited. No part of this publication may be transmitted, stored, or recorded in any form without written permission from the publisher.

Table of Contents

Table of Contents *(cont.)*

Introduction

Why This Book?

We developed this book in response to teachers' needs for good texts to teach reading fluency. In the past several years, reading fluency has become recognized as an essential element in elementary and middle grade reading programs (National Reading Panel, 2001). Readers who are fluent are better able to comprehend what they read - they decode words so effortlessly that they can devote their cognitive resources to the all-important task of comprehension. Fluent readers also construct meaning by reading with appropriate expression and phrasing.

Readers develop fluency through guided practice or repeated readings - reading a text selection several times to the point where it can be expressed meaningfully, with appropriate expression and phrasing. Readers who engage in regular repeated readings, under the guidance and assistance of a teacher or other coach, improve their word recognition, reading rate, comprehension, and overall reading proficiency.

What sorts of texts lend themselves to repeated practice? To us, texts meant to be performed or read orally for an audience are ideal texts for guided repeated reading and reading fluency development. Our goal in this book has been to collect age-appropriate texts meant to be performed or read aloud by students. We have found texts that are relatively short so they can be read and reread in brief periods of time. These texts are from a variety of genre — poetry and rhymes; song lyrics; famous speeches and quotations; Reader's Theater scripts; and other texts such as jokes, cheers, and well wishes. These delightful texts are often neglected in the regular reading program that focuses largely on narrative and informational texts. The passages in this book are also part of our cultural heritage and are important parts of the cultural literacy curriculum for elementary students. Even if you are not teaching reading fluency, your students should read the texts in this book as part of their cultural heritage.

Students will find the texts in this book enjoyable and engaging. They will want to practice reading these texts because of their engaging qualities— the language patterns, the rhyme, the melody, and the inspiration they provide. They will especially want to practice the texts if you provide regular opportunities for your students to perform the texts for their classmates, parents, and other audiences.

Have fun with these texts. Read them with your students again and again. Be assured that if your students regularly read and perform the texts in this book they will begin to develop into fluent readers who are able to decode words effortlessly and construct meaning through their oral interpretation of texts.

Introduction *(cont.)*

How to Use This Book

The texts in this book are engaging and enjoyable. Students will want to read, reread, and perform these texts. As they do, they will develop into fluent readers, improving their ability to recognize words accurately and effortlessly and reading with meaningful expression and phrasing. However, you, the teacher, are the most important part in developing instruction that uses these texts. In this section we recommend ways you can use the texts with your students.

Scheduling and Practice

The texts need to be read repeatedly over several days. We recommend you introduce one text at a time and practice it over the next three, four, or five days, depending on how quickly your students develop mastery over the texts. Write the text you are going to teach on chart paper and/or put it on an overhead transparency.

Read the text with your students several times each day. Read it a few times at the beginning of each day; read it several times during various breaks in the day; and read it multiple times at the end of each day.

Make two copies of the text for each student. Have students keep one copy at school in a "fluency folder." The other copy can be sent home for students to continue practicing the text with their families. Communicate to families the importance of children continuing to practice the text at home with their parents and other family members.

Coaching Your Students

A key ingredient to repeated reading is the coaching that comes from you, the teacher. As your students practice reading the target text each week—alone, in small groups, or as an entire class—be sure to provide positive feedback about their reading. Through oral interpretation of a text readers can express joy, sadness, anger, surprise, or any of a variety of emotions. Help students learn to convey emotion and meaning in their oral reading.

You can do this by listening from time to time to students read and coaching them in the various aspects of oral interpretation. You may wish to suggest that students emphasize certain words, insert dramatic pauses, read a bit faster in one place, or slow down in other parts of the text. And, of course, lavish praise on students' best efforts to convey meaning through their reading. Although it may take a while for students to develop this sense of "voice" in their reading, in the long run it will lead to more engaged and fluent reading and higher levels of comprehension.

Introduction *(cont.)*

Word Study

Although the aim of the fluency texts in this book is to develop fluent and meaningful oral reading of texts, the practicing of passages should also provide opportunities to develop students' vocabulary and word decoding skills. Students may practice a passage repeatedly to the point where it is largely memorized. At this point, students may not look at the words in the text as closely as they should. By continually drawing attention to words in the text, you can help students maintain their focus and develop an ongoing fascination with words.

After reading a passage several times through, ask students to choose words from the passage that they think are interesting. Put these words on a word wall or ask students to add them to their personal word banks. Talk about the meaning of each word and its spelling construction. Help students develop a deepened appreciation for these words and encourage them to use these words in their oral and written language. You might, for example, ask students to use some of the chosen words in their daily journal entries.

Once a list of words has been added to your classroom word wall or students' word banks, play games with the words. One of our favorites is "word bingo." Here, students are given a card with a grid of 3 x 3, 4 x 4, or 5 x 5 boxes. In each box students randomly write a word from the word wall or bank. Then, the teacher calls out definitions of the target words or sentences that contain the target words. Students find the words on their cards and cover them with a marker. Once a horizontal, vertical, or diagonal line of words is covered, they call "Bingo" and win the game.

Have students sort the chosen words along a variety of dimensions—by number of syllables, part of speech, phonics features such as long vowel sound or a consonant blend, or by meaning (e.g., words that can express how a person can feel and words that can't). Through sorting and categorizing activities students get repeated exposure to words, all the time examining the words in different ways.

Help students expand their vocabularies with extended word family instruction. Choose a word from the texts, like "hat", and brainstorm with students other words that belong to the same word family (e.g., "cat," "bat," "chat," etc.). Once a list of family words is chosen, have students create short poems using the rhyming words. These composed poems can be used for further practice and performance. No matter how you do it, make the opportunity to examine select words from the fluency passages part of your regular instructional routine for the fluency texts. The time spent in word study will most definitely be time very well spent.

Introduction *(cont.)*

Performance

After several days of practice, arrange a special time of a day for students to perform the texts. This performance time can range from 5 minutes to 30 minutes depending on the number of texts to be read. Find a special person to listen to your children perform. You may also want to invite a neighboring class, parents, or another group to come to your room to listen to your students read. Have the children perform the targeted text as a group. Later, you can have individuals or groups of children perform the text again.

As an alternative to having your children perform for a group that comes to your room, you may want to send students to visit other adults and children in the building and perform for them. Principals, school secretaries, and visitors to the building are usually great audiences for children's reading. Tape recording and video taping your students' reading is another way to create a performance opportunity.

Regardless of how you accomplish it, it is important that you create the opportunity for your students to perform for some audience. The magic of the performance will give students the motivation to want to practice their assigned texts.

Performance, Not Memorization

Remember, the key to developing fluency is guided reading practice. Students become more fluent when they read the text repeatedly. Reading requires students to actually see the words in the text. Thus, it is important that you do not require students to memorize the text they are practicing and performing. Memorization leads students away from the visualization of the words. Although students may want to try to memorize some texts, our instructional emphasis needs to be on reading with expression so that any audience will enjoy the students' oral rendering of the text. Keep students' eyes on the text whenever possible.

Introduction *(cont.)*

Reader's Theater

Reader's Theater is an exciting and easy method of providing students with an opportunity to practice fluency leading to a performance. Because Reader's Theater minimizes the use of props, sets, costumes, and memorization, it is an easy way to present a "play" in the classroom. Students read from a book or prepared script using their voices to bring the text to life.

Reader's Theater is a communication form that establishes contact with the audience. In traditional drama, the audience is ignored as they watch the characters perform. Reader's Theater, on the other hand, has the following characteristics:

- The script is always read and never memorized.

- Readers may be characters, narrators, or switch back and forth into various characters and parts.

- The readers may sit, stand, or both, but they do not have to perform any other actions.

- Readers use only the interpreter's tools to express emotion. These are eye contact, facial expressions, and vocal expression. The voice, especially, should be very expressive.

- Scripts may be from books, songs, poems, letters, etc. They can be performed directly from the original material or adapted specifically for the Reader's Theater performance.

- Musical accompaniment or soundtracks may be used, but is not necessary.

- Very simple props may be used, especially with younger children, to help the audience identify the parts.

Practice for the Reader's Theater should consist of coached repeated readings that lead to a smooth, fluent presentation.

Websites and Resources for Fluency and Fluency Texts

http://www.theteachersguide.com/ChildrensSongs.htm — children's songs

http://www.niehs.nih.gov/kids/musicchild.htm — children's songs

http://www.gigglepoetry.com – fun and silly poetry

http://loiswalker.com/catalog/guidesamples.html — various scripts

http://www.ruyasonic.com/rdr_edu.htm — information on writing radio drama scripts

http://www.ruyasonic.com/at_kids.htm — information on writing radio drama scripts for children

http://www.margiepalatini.com/readerstheater.html — Reader's Theater scripts

http://www.aaronshep.com/rt/ — Reader's Theater resource

http://www.storycart.com — Reader's Theater scripts (5 free)

Note: These websites were active at the time of publication. As you know sites frequently change, so we cannot guarantee that they will always be available or at the same location.

Poetry and Rhymes

Curly Locks, Curly Locks

Curly Locks, Curly Locks,
Will you be mine?
You shall not wash dishes,
Nor feed the swine,
But sit on a cushion
And sew a fine seam,
And sup upon strawberries,
Sugar, and cream.

Wee Willie Winkie

Wee Willie Winkie
Runs through the town,
Upstairs and downstairs
In his nightgown,
Rapping at the windows,
Crying through the lock,
"Are all the children in their
    beds?
For it's now eight o'clock."

One, Two, Three, Four, Five

One, two, three, four, five,
   Once I caught a fish alive;
Six, seven, eight, nine, ten,
   Then I let it go again.
Why did you let it go?
   Because it bit my finger so.
Which finger did it bite?
   This little finger on my right.

One, Two, Three, Four

One, two, three, four,
Who are we for?
Our school, our school,
　　Rah, rah, rah!

Five, six, seven, eight,
Who do we appreciate?
Our teacher, our teacher,
　　Rah, rah, rah!

Substitute the name of your school for "Our School."

Substitute for "our teacher" the name of the teacher or principal, or any other person you wish to salute in this cheer.

Hey, Diddle, Diddle

Hey, diddle, diddle,

The cat and the fiddle,

The cow jumped over the moon.

The little dog laughed

To see such sport,

And the dish ran away with the

spoon.

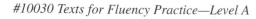

Mary Mary Quite Contrary

Mary, Mary, quite contrary
How does your garden grow?
With silver bells and cockleshells
And pretty maids all in a row.

17

Jack and Jill

Jack and Jill went up the hill
To fetch a pail of water.
Jack fell down and broke his
  crown,
And Jill came tumbling after.

 ©*Shell Educational Publishing*

My Son Ted

By Timothy Rasinski

Diddle diddle dumpling,
    my son Ted
Had a fever so I sent him
    to bed.
Chicken noodle soup is all
    that he's fed.
Diddle diddle dumpling,
    my son Ted.

Inside, Outside, Upside Down

By Timothy Rasinski

Inside, outside, upside down.
Touch your nose, then turn
around.
Jump for joy, then touch the
ground.
Inside, outside, upside down.

Inside, outside, upside down.
Make a smile, then make a
frown.
Go to the country, go to the
town.
Inside, outside, upside down.

Bubble Gum

Bubble gum, bubble gum,
chew and blow.
Bubble gum, bubble gum,
scrape your toe.
Bubble gum, bubble gum,
tastes so sweet.
Get that bubble gum
off your feet!

Snug in a Rug

By Timothy Rasinski

A boy, a bear, and a bug
All rolled up in a rug.
To get out of the rug,
The boy gave a tug
And the bear made a shrug,
But the bug was still snug in
    that rug!

Hickory Dickory Dock

Hickory, dickory, dock!

Tick tock.

The mouse ran up the clock;

Tick tock.

The clock struck one,

The mouse ran down,

Hickory, dickory, dock!

Tick tock.

This could be performed by a group, with one voice reading
the main poem and a group reading the "tick tocks."

Old King Cole

Old King Cole was a merry old soul,
And a merry old soul was he.

He called for his pipe, and he called
    for his bowl,
And he called for his fiddlers three.

Every fiddler had a fiddle fine,
And a very fine fiddle had he, had
    he.

Tweedle dum, tweedle dee, went the
    fiddlers three,
Tweedle dum dee, dum dee deedle
    dee.

The Chair

By Timothy Rasinski

A bug, a boy, and a bear

Sat themselves in the very
same chair.

The chair was too small.

It would not hold them all,

That bug, that boy, and
that bear.

One, Two, Buckle My Shoe

One, two,
Buckle my shoe.

Three, four,
Shut the door.

Five, six,
Pick up sticks.

Seven eight,
Lay them straight.

Nine, ten,
Do it again.

The Queen of Hearts

The Queen of Hearts,
She made some tarts
All on a summer's day.

The Knave of Hearts,
He stole the tarts
And took them clean away.

The King of Hearts,
Called for the tarts
And beat the Knave full sore.

The Knave of Hearts,
Brought back the tarts
And vowed he'd steal no more.

Teddy Bear, Teddy Bear

Teddy bear, Teddy bear,
Turn around.
Teddy bear, Teddy bear,
Touch the ground.

Teddy bear, Teddy bear,
Show your shoe.
Teddy bear, Teddy bear,
That will do.

Teddy bear, Teddy bear,
Run upstairs.
Teddy bear, Teddy bear,
Say your prayers.

Teddy bear, Teddy bear,
Blow out the light.
Teddy bear, Teddy bear,
Say good night.

Old Mother Hubbard

Old Mother Hubbard
Went to the cupboard
To fetch her poor dog a bone;

But when she got there
The cupboard was bare,
And so the poor dog had none.

Another Silly Rhyme

Moses supposes his toeses are
    roses,
But Moses supposes erroneously;

For nobody's toeses are posies
    or roses
As Moses supposes his toeses to
    be.

Pickles

By Timothy Rasinski

Sweet pickles, dill pickles

tickle my tongue.

Eat them on bread

or a hamburger bun.

A pickle sandwich

is so much fun.

Sweet pickles, dill pickles

tickle my tongue.

Star Light, Star Bright

Star light, star bright,

First star I see tonight,

I wish I may, I wish I might,

Have the wish I wish tonight.

I'm Glad

I'm glad the sky is painted blue

And the earth is painted green.

With such a lot of nice fresh air

All sandwiched in between.

Hiking Home

By Timothy Rasinski

Willy and Billy took a hike

With their buddy Silly Mike.

Up and down the hills they
roamed.

Till three tired friends came
hiking home.

Kitty Cat

By Timothy Rasinski

Pitty pat, pitty pat,

Here comes my kitty cat.

A ball of fluff, plump and fat,

Full of fun, my kitty cat.

Miss Polly Had a Dolly

Miss Polly had a dolly,

Who was sick, sick, sick,

So she called for a doctor

To come quick, quick, quick.

The doctor came with his bag and
his cap,

And he knocked on the door with
a rat a tat tap.

He looked at the dolly,

And he shook his head,

And said, "Miss Polly, put her
straight to bed."

He wrote on a paper for a pill,
pill, pill,

I'll be back in the morning with
my bill, bill, bill.

Summer's Over

By Timothy Rasinski

Summer's over;

Close the pool.

Summer's over;

Time for school.

Summer's over;

Books are cool.

Summer's over;

Teachers rule!

Higglety, Pigglety

Higglety, pigglety, my black hen,

She lays eggs for gentlemen.

Gentlemen come every day

To see what my black hen doth
lay.

Sometimes nine, and sometimes
ten.

Higglety, pigglety, my black hen.

The Swing

By Robert Louis Stevenson

How do you like to go up in a swing,
Up in the air so blue?
Oh, I do think it the pleasantest thing
Ever a child can do!

Up in the air and over the wall,
Till I can see so wide,
Rivers and trees and cattle and all
Over the countryside—

Till I look down on the garden green,
Down on the roof so brown—
Up in the air I go flying again,
Up in the air and down!

The Purple Cow

By Gelett Burgess

I never saw a purple cow.

I never hope to see one;

But I can tell you, anyhow,

I'd rather see than be one!

Little Boy Blue

Little Boy Blue,
Come blow your horn!
The sheep's in the meadow,
The cow's in the corn.

Where is the little boy
Tending the sheep?
He's under the haystack,
Fast asleep.

Will you wake him?
No, not I;
For if I do,
He's sure to cry.

Wynken, Blynken, and Nod

By Eugene Field

Wynken, Blynken, and Nod one night
Sailed off in a wooden shoe—
Sailed on a river of crystal light,
Into a sea of dew.
"Where are you going, and what do you
    wish?"
The old moon asked the three.
"We have come to fish for the herring fish
That live in this beautiful sea;
Nets of silver and gold have we!"
Said Wynken, Blynken, and Nod.

The old moon laughed and sang a song,
As they rocked in the wooden shoe,
And the wind that sped them all night long
Ruffled the waves of dew.
The little stars were the herring fish
That lived in the beautiful sea.
"Now cast your nets wherever you wish—
Never afraid are we!"
So cried the stars to the fishermen three:
Wynken, Blynken, and Nod.

Wynken, Blynken, and Nod *(cont.)*

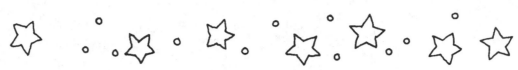

All night long their nets they threw
To the stars in the twinkling foam—
Then down from the skies came the
    wooden shoe,
Bringing the fishermen home;
'Twas all so pretty a sail it seemed
As if it could not be;
And some folk thought 'twas a dream
    they'd dreamed
Of sailing that beautiful sea—
But I shall name you the fishermen three:
Wynken, Blynken, and Nod.

Wynken and Blynken are two little eyes,
And Nod is a little head,
And the wooden shoe that sailed the skies
Is a wee one's trundle-bed.
So shut your eyes while Mother sings
Of wonderful sights that be,
And you shall see the beautiful things
As you rock in the misty sea,
Where the old shoe rocked the fishermen
    three—
Wynken, Blynken, and Nod.

Three Little Kittens

Three little kittens lost their mittens,
And they began to cry,
"Oh, mother dear, we sadly fear,
Our mittens we have lost!"

"What! Lost your mittens?
You naughty kittens!
Then you shall have no pie."
"Meow, meow, meow!"
"No, you shall have no pie."

Three little kittens found their mittens,
And they began to cry,
"Oh, mother dear, see here, see here,
Our mittens we have found!"

"What! Found your mittens?
You good little kittens!
Then you shall have some pie."
"Meow, meow, meow."
"Yes, you shall have some pie."

*NOTE: This poem is also available, with additional verses, in the
Reader's Theater section on page 102–103.*

To Market, To Market

To market, to market, to buy a
fat pig.

Home again, home again,
jiggety-jig;

To market, to market, to buy a
fat hog,

Home again, home again,
jiggety-jog.

Spring

By William Blake

Sound the flute!
Now it's mute!
Birds delight,
Day and night,
Nightingale,
In the dale,
Lark in sky,
Merrily,
Merrily, merrily to welcome in the year.

Little boy,
Full of joy;
Little girl,
Sweet and small;
Cock does crow,
So do you;
Merry voice,
Infant noise;
Merrily, merrily to welcome in the year.

Little lamb,
Here I am;
Come and lick
My white neck;
Let me pull
Your soft wool;
Let me kiss
Your soft face;
Merrily, merrily we welcome in the year.

Song Lyrics

A Hunting We Will Go

A hunting we will go, a hunting we will go
Heigh ho, the dairy-o, a hunting we will go
A hunting we will go, a hunting we will go
We'll catch a fox and put him in a box
And then we'll let him go

A hunting we will go, a hunting we will go
Heigh ho, the dairy-o, a hunting we will go
A hunting we will go, a hunting we will go
We'll catch a fish and put him on a dish
And then we'll let him go

A hunting we will go, a hunting we will go
Heigh ho, the dairy-o, a hunting we will go
A hunting we will go, a hunting we will go
We'll catch a bear and cut his hair
And then we'll let him go

A hunting we will go, a hunting we will go
Heigh ho, the dairy-o, a hunting we will go
A hunting we will go, a hunting we will go
We'll catch a pig and dance a little jig
And then we'll let him go

A hunting we will go, a hunting we will go
Heigh ho, the dairy-o, a hunting we will go
A hunting we will go, a hunting we will go
We'll catch a giraffe and make him laugh
And then we'll let him go.

This Old Man

1

This old man, he played one,
He played knick knack on my thumb,
With a knick, knack, paddy whack,
Give the dog a bone;
This old man came rolling home.

2

This old man, he played two,
He played knick knack on my shoe,
With a knick, knack, paddy whack,
Give the dog a bone;
This old man came rolling home.

3

This old man, he played three,
He played knick knack on my knee,
With a knick, knack, paddy whack,
Give the dog a bone;
This old man came rolling home.

This Old Man (cont.)

4

This old man, he played four,
He played knick knack at my door,
With a knick, knack, paddy whack,
Give the dog a bone;
This old man came rolling home.

5

This old man, he played five,
He played knick knack, jazz and jive,
With a knick, knack, paddy whack,
Give the dog a bone;
This old man came rolling home.

6

This old man, he played six,
He played knick knack with his sticks,
With a knick, knack, paddy whack,
Give the dog a bone;
This old man came rolling home.

This Old Man *(cont.)*

7

This old man, he played seven,
He played knick knack with his pen,
With a knick, knack, paddy whack,
Give the dog a bone;
This old man came rolling home.

8

This old man, he played eight,
He played knick knack on my gate,
With a knick, knack, paddy whack,
Give the dog a bone;
This old man came rolling home.

9

This old man, he played nine,
He played knick knack, rise and shine,
With a knick, knack, paddy whack,
Give the dog a bone;
This old man came rolling home.

This Old Man *(cont.)*

10

This old man, he played ten,
He played knick knack in my den,
With a knick, knack, paddy whack,
Give the dog a bone;
This old man came rolling home.

11

This old man, he played eleven,
He played knick knack up in heaven,
With a knick, knack, paddy whack,
Give the dog a bone;
This old man came rolling home.

12

This old man, he played twelve,
He played knick knack, dig and delve,
With a knick, knack, paddy whack,
Give the dog a bone;
This old man came rolling home.

Pop Goes the Weasel

Round and round the cobbler's bench
The monkey chased the weasel,
The monkey thought 'twas all in fun
Pop! Goes the weasel.

A penny for a spool of thread
A penny for a needle,
That's the way the money goes,
Pop! Goes the weasel.

A half a pound of tupenny rice,
A half a pound of treacle.
Mix it up and make it nice,
Pop! Goes the weasel.

Pop Goes the Weasel *(cont.)*

Up and down the London road,
In and out of the Eagle,
That's the way the money goes,
Pop! Goes the weasel.

Johnny's got the whooping cough,
Mary's got the measles,
Call the doctor to come quick,
Pop! Goes the weasel.

I've no time to plead and pine,
I've no time to wheedle,
Kiss me quick and then I'm gone
Pop! Goes the weasel.

The Itsy Bitsy Spider

The itsy bitsy spider
Went up the water spout.
Down came the rain
And washed the spider out.

Out came the sun
And dried up all the rain
And the itsy bitsy spider
Went up the spout again.

Baa, Baa, Black Sheep

Baa, baa, black sheep,
Have you any wool?
Yes sir, yes sir,
Three bags full.

One for the master,
One for the dame,
And one for the little boy
Who lives down the lane.

Baa, baa, black sheep,
Have you any wool?
Yes sir, yes sir,
Three bags full.

Bingo

There was a farmer had a dog,
And Bingo was his name-o.
B-I-N-G-O!
B-I-N-G-O!
B-I-N-G-O!
And Bingo was his name-o!

There was a farmer had a dog,
And Bingo was his name-o.
(Clap)-I-N-G-O!
(Clap)-I-N-G-O!
(Clap)-I-N-G-O!
And Bingo was his name-o!

There was a farmer had a dog,
And Bingo was his name-o.
(Clap, clap)-N-G-O!
(Clap, clap)-N-G-O!
(Clap, clap)-N-G-O!
And Bingo was his name-o!

Bingo *(cont.)*

There was a farmer had a dog,
And Bingo was his name-o.
(Clap, clap, clap)-G-O!
(Clap, clap, clap)-G-O!
(Clap, clap, clap)-G-O!
And Bingo was his name-o!

There was a farmer had a dog,
And Bingo was his name-o.
(Clap, clap, clap, clap)-O!
(Clap, clap, clap, clap)-O!
(Clap, clap, clap, clap)-O!
And Bingo was his name-o!

There was a farmer had a dog,
And Bingo was his name-o.
(Clap, clap, clap, clap, clap)
(Clap, clap, clap, clap, clap)
(Clap, clap, clap, clap, clap)
And Bingo was his name-o!

Yankee Doodle

Yankee Doodle went to town
A-riding on a pony
Stuck a feather in his hat
And called it macaroni.

Yankee Doodle, keep it up,
Yankee Doodle dandy,
Mind the music and the step
And with the girls be handy.

The Farmer in the Dell

The farmer in the dell,
The farmer in the dell,
Hi-ho, the derry-o
The farmer in the dell.

The farmer takes a wife;
The farmer takes a wife;
Hi-ho, the derry-o
The farmer takes a wife.

The wife takes a child;
The wife takes a child;
Hi-ho, the derry-o
The wife takes a child.

The child takes a nurse;
The child takes a nurse;
Hi-ho, the derry-o
The child takes a nurse.

The nurse takes a cow;
The nurse takes a cow;
Hi-ho, the derry-o
The nurse takes a cow.

The Farmer in the Dell *(cont.)*

The cow takes a dog;
The cow takes a dog;
Hi-ho, the derry-o
The cow takes a dog.

The dog takes a cat;
The dog takes a cat;
Hi-ho, the derry-o
The dog takes a cat.

The cat takes a rat;
The cat takes a rat;
Hi-ho, the derry-o
The cat takes a rat.

The rat takes the cheese;
The rat takes the cheese;
Hi-ho, the derry-o
The rat takes the cheese.

The cheese stands alone;
The cheese stands alone;
Hi-ho, the derry-o
The cheese stands alone.

London Bridge

London Bridge is falling down,
Falling down, falling down.
London Bridge is falling down,
My fair lady!

Build it up with iron bars,
Iron bars, iron bars.
Build it up with iron bars,
My fair lady!

Iron bars will bend and break,
Bend and break, bend and break.
Iron bars will bend and break,
My fair lady!

Build it up with needles and pins,
Needles and pins, needles and pins.
Build it up with needles and pins,
My fair lady!

Pins and needles will rust and bend,
Rust and bend, rust and bend.
Pins and needles will rust and bend,
My fair lady!

London Bridge *(cont.)*

Build it up with penny loaves,
Penny loaves, penny loaves.
Build it up with penny loaves,
My fair lady!

Penny loaves will tumble down,
Tumble down, tumble down.
Penny loaves will tumble down,
My fair lady!

Build it up with silver and gold,
Silver and gold, silver and gold.
Build it up with silver and gold,
My fair lady!

Gold and silver we do not have,
Do not have, do not have.
Gold and silver we do not have,
My fair lady!

There's a prisoner you do have,
You do have, you do have.
There's a prisoner you do have,
My fair lady!

London Bridge *(cont.)*

What'll you take to set him free,
Set him free, set him free?
What'll you take to set him free?
My fair lady!

One hundred dollars will set him free,
Set him free, set him free.
One hundred dollars will set him free,
My fair lady!

One hundred dollars we do not have,
Do not have, do not have.
One hundred dollars we do not have,
My fair lady!

Then off to prison he must go,
He must go, he must go.
Off to prison he must go,
My fair lady!

Mary Had a Little Lamb

Mary had a little lamb,
Little lamb, little lamb,
Mary had a little lamb,
Its fleece was white as snow.

Everywhere that Mary went,
Mary went, Mary went,
Everywhere that Mary went
The lamb was sure to go.

It followed her to school one day,
School one day, school one day,
It followed her to school one day
Which was against the rules.

It made the children laugh and play,
Laugh and play, laugh and play,
It made the children laugh and play
To see a lamb at school.

Jingle Bells

Jingle bells, jingle bells,
Jingle all the way.
Oh, what fun it is to ride
In a one-horse open sleigh! Hey!

Jingle bells, jingle bells,
Jingle all the way.
Oh, what fun it is to ride
In a one-horse open sleigh!

Old MacDonald

Old MacDonald had a farm,
Ee-i-ee-i-oh!
And on his farm he had some hens,
Ee-i-ee-i-oh!
With a cluck-cluck here,
And a cluck-cluck there,
Here a cluck, there a cluck,
Everywhere a cluck-cluck.
Old MacDonald had a farm
Ee-i-ee-i-oh!

Old MacDonald had a farm,
Ee-i-ee-i-oh!
And on his farm he had some cows,
Ee-i-ee-i-oh!
With a moo-moo here,
And a moo-moo there,
Here a moo, there a moo,
Everywhere a moo-moo.
Old MacDonald had a farm,
Ee-i-ee-i-oh!

Old MacDonald *(cont.)*

Old MacDonald had a farm,
Ee-i-ee-i-oh!
And on his farm he had some pigs,
Ee-i-ee-i-oh!
With an oink-oink here,
And an oink-oink there,
Here an oink, there an oink,
Everywhere an oink-oink.
Old MacDonald had a farm
Ee-i-ee-i-oh!

Old MacDonald had a farm,
Ee-i-ee-i-oh!
And on his farm he had some horses,
Ee-i-ee-i-oh!
With an neigh, neigh here,
And an neigh, neigh there,
Here an neigh, there an neigh,
Everywhere an neigh, neigh.
Old MacDonald had a farm
Ee-i-ee-i-oh!

Polly Wolly Doodle

Oh, I went down South
For to see my Sal;
Sing Polly wolly doodle all the day.
My Sal, she is a spunky gal;
Sing Polly wolly doodle all the day.

Fare thee well, fare thee well,
Fare thee well my fairy fay,
I'm going to Lou'siana
For to see my Susyanna,
Sing Polly wolly doodle all the day.

Oh, my Sal, she is a maiden fair;
Sing Polly wolly doodle all the day.
With curly eyes and laughing hair;
Sing Polly wolly doodle all the day.

Fare thee well, fare thee well,
Fare thee well my fairy fay,
I'm going to Lou'siana
For to see my Susyanna,
Sing Polly wolly doodle all the day.

Row, Row, Row Your Boat

Row, row, row your boat

Gently down the stream.

Merrily, merrily, merrily, merrily,

Life is but a dream.

 ©Shell Edcational Publishing

Skip to My Lou

Fly's in the buttermilk,
Shoo, fly, shoo.
Fly's in the buttermilk,
Shoo, fly, shoo.
Fly's in the buttermilk,
Shoo, fly, shoo.
Skip to my Lou, my darlin.

Skip, skip, skip to my Lou,
Skip, skip, skip to my Lou,
Skip, skip, skip to my Lou,
Skip to my Lou, my darlin.

Cat's in the cream jar,
Ooh, ooh, ooh,
Cat's in the cream jar,
Ooh, ooh, ooh,
Cat's in the cream jar,
Ooh, ooh, ooh,
Skip to my Lou, my darlin.

Skip, skip, skip to my Lou,
Skip, skip, skip to my Lou,
Skip, skip, skip to my Lou,
Skip to my Lou, my darlin.

Skip to My Lou (cont.)

Cows in the cornfield,
What'll I do?
Cows in the cornfield,
What'll I do?
Cows in the cornfield,
What'll I do?
Skip to my Lou, my darlin.

Skip, skip, skip to my Lou,
Skip, skip, skip to my Lou,
Skip, skip, skip to my Lou,
Skip to my Lou, my darlin.

There's a little red wagon,
Paint it blue.
There's a little red wagon,
Paint it blue.
There's a little red wagon,
Paint it blue.
Skip to my Lou, my darlin.

Skip, skip, skip to my Lou,
Skip, skip, skip to my Lou,
Skip, skip, skip to my Lou,
Skip to my Lou, my darlin.

Skip to My Lou *(cont.)*

Lost my partner,
What'll I do?
Lost my partner,
What'll I do?
Lost my partner,
What'll I do?
Skip to my Lou, my darlin.

Skip, skip, skip to my Lou,
Skip, skip, skip to my Lou,
Skip, skip, skip to my Lou,
Skip to my Lou, my darlin.

I'll get another one
See if I do.
I'll get another one
See if I do.
I'll get another one
See if I do.
Skip to my Lou, my darlin.

Skip, skip, skip to my Lou,
Skip, skip, skip to my Lou,
Skip, skip, skip to my Lou,
Skip to my Lou, my darlin.

Camptown Races

By Stephen Foster

The Camptown ladies
sing this song,

Doo-da, Doo-da.

The Camptown racetrack's
five miles long

Oh, de doo-da day.

Goin' to run all night,

Goin' to run all day.

I bet my money on a bob-
tailed nag,

Somebody bet on the gray.

The Ants Go Marching

The ants go marching one by one, hurrah, hurrah.
The ants go marching one by one, hurrah, hurrah.
The ants go marching one by one,
The little one stops to suck his thumb,
And they all go marching down to the ground
To get out of the rain, BOOM! BOOM! BOOM!

The ants go marching two by two, hurrah, hurrah.
The ants go marching two by two, hurrah, hurrah.
The ants go marching two by two,
The little one stops to tie his shoe,
And they all go marching down to the ground
To get out of the rain, BOOM! BOOM! BOOM!

The ants go marching three by three, hurrah, hurrah.
The ants go marching three by three, hurrah, hurrah.
The ants go marching three by three,
The little one stops to climb a tree,
And they all go marching down to the ground
To get out of the rain, BOOM! BOOM! BOOM!

The Ants Go Marching *(cont.)*

The ants go marching four by four, hurrah, hurrah.
The ants go marching four by four, hurrah, hurrah.
The ants go marching four by four,
The little one stops to shut the door,
And they all go marching down to the ground
To get out of the rain, BOOM! BOOM! BOOM!

The ants go marching five by five, hurrah, hurrah.
The ants go marching five by five, hurrah, hurrah.
The ants go marching five by five,
The little one stops to take a dive,
And they all go marching down to the ground
To get out of the rain, BOOM! BOOM! BOOM!

The ants go marching six by six, hurrah, hurrah.
The ants go marching six by six, hurrah, hurrah.
The ants go marching six by six,
The little one stops to pick up sticks,
And they all go marching down to the ground
To get out of the rain, BOOM! BOOM! BOOM!

The Ants Go Marching (cont.)

The ants go marching seven by seven, hurrah,
   hurrah.
The ants go marching seven by seven, hurrah,
   hurrah.
The ants go marching seven by seven,
The little one stops to pray to heaven,
And they all go marching down to the ground
To get out of the rain, BOOM! BOOM! BOOM!

The ants go marching eight by eight, hurrah, hurrah.
The ants go marching eight by eight, hurrah, hurrah.
The ants go marching eight by eight,
The little one stops to shut the gate,
And they all go marching down to the ground
To get out of the rain, BOOM! BOOM! BOOM!

The ants go marching nine by nine, hurrah, hurrah.
The ants go marching nine by nine, hurrah, hurrah.
The ants go marching nine by nine,
The little one stops to check the time,
And they all go marching down to the ground
To get out of the rain, BOOM! BOOM! BOOM!

The ants go marching ten by ten, hurrah, hurrah.
The ants go marching ten by ten, hurrah, hurrah.
The ants go marching ten by ten,
The little one stops to say "THE END,"
And they all go marching down to the ground
To get out of the rain, BOOM! BOOM! BOOM!

Love Somebody

Love somebody, yes I do,
Love somebody, yes I do,
Love somebody, yes I do,
And I hope somebody loves me too.

Love somebody, can't guess who,
Love somebody, can't guess who,
Love somebody, can't guess who,
And I hope somebody loves me too.

If You're Happy and You Know It

If you're happy and you know it,
Clap your hands.
If you're happy and you know it,
Clap your hands.
If you're happy and you know it,
Then your face will surely show it,
If you're happy and you know it,
Clap your hands.

If you're happy and you know it,
Stomp your feet.
If you're happy and you know it,
Stomp your feet.
If you're happy and you know it,
Then your face will surely show it,
If you're happy and you know it,
Stomp your feet.

If You're Happy and You Know It *(cont.)*

If you're happy and you know it,
  Shout "Hurray!"
If you're happy and you know it,
  Shout "Hurray!"
If you're happy and you know it,
Then your face will surely show it,
If you're happy and you know it,
  Shout "Hurray!"

If you're happy and you know it,
  Do all three.
If you're happy and you know it,
  Do all three.
If you're happy and you know it,
Then your face will surely show it,
If you're happy and you know it,
  Do all three.

Smiles

By J. Will Callahan

There are smiles that make us
    happy,

There are smiles that make us blue,

There are smiles that steal away
    the tear-drops,

As the sunbeams steal away the
    dew.

There are smiles that have a tender
meaning

That the eyes of love alone may
    see,

And the smiles that fill my life with
sunshine

Are the smiles that you give to me.

The Seventh Silly Rhyme

I went to the animal fair,

The birds and beasts were there.

The big baboon, by the light of
the moon,

Was combing his auburn hair.

The monkey, he got drunk,

And sat on the elephant's trunk.

The elephant sneezed and fell on
his knees,

And what became of the monk,
the monk?

Wheels on the Bus

The wheels on the bus go round and round,
Round and round,
Round and round.
The wheels on the bus go round and round,
   all through the town.

The wipers on the bus go swish, swish, swish,
Swish, swish, swish,
Swish, swish, swish.
The wipers on the bus go swish, swish, swish,
   all through the town.

The horn on the bus goes beep, beep, beep,
Beep, beep, beep,
Beep, beep, beep.
The horn on the bus goes beep, beep, beep,
   all through the town.

The money on the bus goes, clink, clink, clink,
Clink, clink, clink,
Clink, clink, clink.
The money on the bus goes, clink, clink, clink,
   all through the town.

Wheels on the Bus *(cont.)*

The driver on the bus says, "Move on back,
Move on back,
Move on back."
The driver on the bus says, "Move on back,"
    all through the town.

The people on the bus say, "Here's a seat,
Here's a seat,
Here's a seat."
The people on the bus say, "Here's a seat,"
    all through the town.

The baby on the bus says, "Wah, wah, wah,
Wah, wah, wah,
Wah, wah, wah."
The baby on the bus says, "Wah, wah, wah,"
all through the town.

The mommy on the bus says, "Shush, shush,
    shush,
Shush, shush, shush,
Shush, shush, shush."
The mommy on the bus says, "Shush, shush,
    shush,"
    all through the town.

Do Your Ears Hang Low?

Do your ears hang low?

Do they wobble to and fro?

Can you tie them in a knot?

Can you tie them in a bow?

Can you throw them o'er
your shoulder

like a continental soldier?

Do your ears hang low?

America

My country! 'tis of thee,

Sweet land of liberty,

Of thee I sing;

Land where my fathers died,

Land of the pilgrim's pride,

From every mountain side,

Let freedom ring.

Quotations
&
Monologues

I Thought a Thought

I thought a thought.
But the thought I thought
wasn't the thought
I thought I thought.

A penny saved is a penny earned.

(Benjamin Franklin)

Practice makes perfect.

Do unto others as you would have them do unto you.

It is better to give than to receive.

If at first you don't succeed, try, try again.

A place for everything and everything in its place.

Great oaks from little acorns grow.

Never leave until tomorrow what you can do today.

April showers bring May flowers.

The early bird gets the worm.

An apple a day keeps the doctor away.

One bad apple can spoil the whole barrel.

Haste makes waste.

Don't judge a book by its cover.

Little by little does the trick.

Aesop

A good beginning leads to a good end.

 ©*Shell Edcational Publishing*

Reader's Theater Scripts

Good, Better, Best

For three voices

V1: Good,

V2: Better,

V3: Best!

V1: Never let it rest,

V2: Till the good is better,

V3: And the better is best!

All: YES!
Good, better, best!
Never let it rest,
Till the good is better,
And the better is best!

I'm Nobody

By Emily Dickinson

R1: I'm nobody! Who are you?
Are you nobody, too?

R2: Then there's a pair of us—don't tell!
They'd banish us, you know.

R1: How dreary to be somebody!

R2: How public like a frog.

Both: To tell your name the livelong day
To an admiring bog!

Bananas and Apples

By Lorraine Griffith

A Reader's Theater for the five senses: eyes, hands, nose, ears, tongue

ALL: Bananas

Eyes: I can see a yellow banana.

Hands: I can feel the rubbery peel.

Nose: I can smell its sweet, yummy scent.

Ears: I can hear my cereal crackle when the milk is poured.

Tongue: I can taste the sweet banana-flavored grains.

ALL: I just love my breakfast treat!

ALL: Bananas

ALL: Apples

Eyes: I can see a red shiny apple.

Hands: I can feel its smooth, thin peel.

Nose: I can smell its tart, fruity scent.

Ears: I can hear my mother cutting the apple into wedges.

Tongue: I can taste the sour sweet flavor.

ALL: I just love my afternoon snack!

ALL: Apples

This Reader's Theater could be easily extended by the children's own brainstorming on favorite foods. Wearing a sign picturing the sensory organ makes this fun and very visual for children viewing or participating in the performance.

Johnny Appleseed

By Lorraine Griffith

All: Johnny Appleseed

Reader 1: A famous American

Reader 2: Who planted apple trees

Reader 3: All over America.

All: A dreamer

Reader 2: For a land

Reader 3: With blossoming apple trees

Reader 1: And no one hungry.

All: A kind and gentle man

Reader 3: Slept outdoors

Reader 2: Walked barefoot

Reader 1: Wore a flour sack on his body

Reader 2: And a tin pot on his head.

ALL: Johnny Appleseed,
A famous American
Who planted apple trees
All over America.

The Months

A Traditional Rhyme, Author unknown

A Reader's Theater for 6 voices

ALL: January brings the snow,

Reader 1: Makes our feet and fingers glow.

ALL: February brings the rains,

Reader 2: Thaws the frozen lake again.

ALL: March brings breezes sharp and chill,

Reader 3: Shakes the dancing daffodil.

ALL: April brings the primrose sweet,

Reader 4: Scatters daisies at our feet.

ALL: May brings flocks of pretty lambs,

Reader 5: Sporting round their fleecy dams.

ALL: June brings tulips, lilies, roses,

Reader 6: Fills the children's hands with posies.

ALL: Hot July brings thundershowers,

Reader 1: Apricots, and gillyflowers.

ALL: August brings the sheaves of corn;

Reader 2: Then the harvest home is borne.

ALL: Warm September brings the fruit;

Reader 3: Sportsmen then begin to shoot.

ALL: Brown October brings the pheasant,

Reader 4: Then to gather nuts is pleasant.

ALL: Dull November brings the blast,

Reader 5: Hark! The leaves are whirling fast.

ALL: Cold December brings the sleet,

Reader 6: Blazing fire, and Christmas treat.

Shall I Sing?

A nursery rhyme, author unknown

A Reader's Theater for a lark, a flower, the sun, a shower, and a narrator

Lark:	Shall I sing?
Narrator:	says the Lark,
Flower:	Shall I bloom?
Narrator:	says the Flower;
Sun:	Shall I come?
Narrator:	says the Sun,
Shower:	Or shall I?
Narrator:	says the Shower.
All except Lark:	Sing your song, pretty Bird,
All except Flower:	Roses bloom for an hour;
All except Sun:	Shine on, dearest Sun;
All except Shower:	Go away, naughty Shower.

The Princess and the Pea

By Hans Christian Andersen (1835)
Retold/arranged by Lorraine Griffith

**A Reader's Theater for eight: five readers,
an old king, an old queen, and a princess**

ALL: The Princess and the Pea

Princess: A Fairy Tale

King: by Hans Christian Andersen

Reader 1: Once upon a time there was a prince

Reader 2: who was looking for a real princess to marry.

Reader 3: One evening in a terrible storm,

Reader 4: a knock was heard on the city gate.

Reader 5: The old king came to the gate

Reader 1: and saw a very wet and muddy girl standing there.

King: "Good Gracious!"

Reader 2: The king said, shocked at the sight of the wet and muddy girl.

Princess: "Please allow me to come in, for I am a princess."

Reader 3: The old queen didn't believe her, for she didn't look like a princess.

The Princess and the Pea *(cont.)*

Queen: "Well, we'll soon find that out,"

Reader 4: said the old queen as she went up to the bedroom.

Reader 5: She took all the bedding off the bed,

Reader 1: laid a pea on the bottom,

Reader 2: put twenty mattresses over the pea

Reader 3: and twenty more quilts over the mattress.

Reader 4: The princess climbed up on the bed and had to lie all night long.

Reader 5: In the morning, she was asked by the queen,

Queen: "How did you sleep?"

Princess: "Oh, very badly! I never fell asleep!"

Reader 1: she whined.

Princess: "I was lying on something hard and my whole body is black and blue! It was horrible."

Reader 2: Then they knew she was a real princess!

Reader 3: Nobody but a real princess could feel a pea through

Reader 4: twenty mattresses and twenty quilts.

Reader 5: So the prince found his princess to marry

ALL: and they lived happily ever after.

Three Little Kittens

A Reader's Theater for 3 little kittens, a mother, and a narrator

Narrator: Three little kittens,
They lost their mittens,
And they began to cry,

Kitten 1:   Oh, mother, dear,

Kitten 2:   We sadly fear,

Kitten 3:   Our mittens we have lost.

Mother: What! Lost your mittens,
You naughty kittens,
Then you shall have no pie.

Kittens: Meow, meow, meow!

Mother: Then you shall have no pie.

Narrator: The three little kittens,
They found their mittens,
And they began to cry,

Kitten 1:   Oh, mother, dear,

Kitten 2:   See here, see here,

Kitten 3:   Our mittens we have found.

Mother: What, found your mittens,
Then you're good kittens,
And you shall have some pie.

Kittens: Purr-rr, purr-rr, purr-rr!

Mother: Then you shall have some pie.

Three Little Kittens *(cont.)*

Narrator: Three little kittens,
Put on their mittens,
And soon ate up the pie.

Kitten 1: Oh, mother, dear,

Kitten 2: We sadly fear,

Kitten 3: Our mittens we have soiled.

Mother: What! Soiled your mittens,
You naughty kittens,

Narrator: And they began to sigh.

Kittens: Meow, meow, meow!

Narrator: And they began to sigh.

Narrator: The three little kittens,
They washed their mittens,
And hung them out to dry.

Kitten 1: Oh, mother, dear,

Kitten 2: Do you not hear,

Kitten 3: Our mittens we have washed?

Mother: What! Washed your mittens?
Then you're good kittens!
But I smell a rat close by.

Kittens: Meow, meow, meow!
We smell a rat close by.

One Stormy Night

A Reader's Theater for two readers and two kittens.

Reader 1:	Two little kittens,
Reader 2:	one stormy night,
Reader 1:	began to quarrel
Reader 2:	and then to fight.
Reader 1:	One had a mouse
Reader 2:	and the other had none,
Readers 1 & 2:	and that's the way the quarrel was begun.
Kitten 1:	"I'll have that mouse!"
Reader 1:	said the biggest cat.
Kitten 2:	"You'll have that mouse? We'll see about that!"
Kitten 1:	"I will have that mouse!"
Reader 1:	said the eldest son.
Kitten 2:	"You shall not have the mouse,"
Reader 2:	said the little one.
Reader 1:	I told you before 'twas a stormy night
Reader 2:	when these two little kittens began to fight.
Reader 1:	The old woman seized her sweeping broom,
Reader 2:	and swept the two kittens right out of the room.
Reader 1:	The ground was covered with frost and snow,
Reader 2:	and the two little kittens had nowhere to go;
Reader 1:	So they laid right down on the mat at the door
Reader 2:	while the old woman finished sweeping the floor.
Reader 1:	Then they crept back in as quiet as mice,
Reader 2:	all wet with snow and cold as ice,
Readers 1 & 2:	for they found it was better, that stormy night,
Kittens:	to lie down and sleep than to quarrel and fight.

What Is It?

By Lorraine Griffith

A Reader's Theater for three frightened children!

Reader 1: It is on me!

Reader 2: It is under me!

Reader 3: It is over me!

ALL: WHAT IS IT?

Reader 1: It is in front of me!

Reader 2: It is in back of me!

Reader 3: It is next to me!

ALL: WHAT IS IT?

Reader 1: It is inside of me!

Reader 2: It is outside of me!

Reader 3: It is around me!

ALL: WHAT IS IT?

Reader 1: It is far from me!

Reader 2: It is near me!

Reader 3: It is above me!

ALL: WHAT IS IT?

Reader 1: It is below me!

Reader 2: It is to the right of me!

Reader 3: It is to the left of me!

ALL: WHAT IS IT?

Reader 1: It is here!

Reader 2: It is there!

ALL: WHAT IS IT?

Reader 3: It is AIR!

The Nesting Hour

A nursery rhyme

A Reader's Theater for 2 voices.

Reader 1: Robin-friend has gone to bed,

Reader 2: Little wing to hide his head;

Reader 1: Mother's bird must slumber too,

Reader 2: Just like baby robins do.

ALL: When the stars begin to rise
Birds and babies close their eyes.

The Little Red Hen

Five Parts: Narrator, Hen, Pig, Duck, Cat

Narrator: Once upon a time, a pig, a duck, a cat and a little red hen all lived together in a cozy little house on a pretty green hill. All day long, the pig wallowed happily in its juicy mud puddle, the duck swam happily on her little pond, and the cat slept happily in the sun. This left all the work of the house for the little red hen to do. One day, as the little red hen was scratching about in the yard looking for a nice beetle for her dinner, she came upon a grain of wheat. It gave her an idea.

Hen: Who will plant this grain of wheat?

Narrator: She asked of the pig, the duck, and the cat.

Pig: Not I.

Narrator: Said the pig.

Duck: Not I.

Narrator: Said the duck.

Cat: Not I.

Narrator: Said the cat.

Hen: Then I will do it myself.

Narrator: And she did. The grain of wheat sprouted, and it grew and grew until it was tall and golden and ready to cut.

Hen: Who will cut the wheat?

Narrator: She asked of the pig, the duck, and the cat.

Pig: Not I.

Narrator: Said the pig.

Duck: Not I.

Narrator: Said the duck.

Cat: Not I.

Narrator: Said the cat.

Hen: Then I will do it myself.

Narrator: Said the little red hen, and she did. When the wheat was cut, it was ready to be ground into flour.

Hen: Who will take the wheat to the mill?

Narrator: She asked of the pig, the duck, and the cat.

The Little Red Hen (cont.)

Pig: Not I.

Narrator: Said the pig.

Duck: Not I.

Narrator: Said the duck.

Cat: Not I.

Narrator: Said the cat.

Hen: Then I will do it myself.

Narrator: Said the little red hen, and she did! Soon a little sack of fine flour came back from the mill.

Hen: Who will make the flour into bread?

Narrator: She asked of the pig, the duck, and the cat.

Pig: Not I.

Narrator: Said the pig.

Duck: Not I.

Narrator: Said the duck.

Cat: Not I.

Narrator: Said the cat.

Hen: Then I will do it myself.

Narrator: Said the little red hen, and she did. When the bread was baked, the little red hen took it from the oven. It was the most beautiful, crusty brown loaf she had ever seen.

Hen: Who will eat the bread?

Narrator: She asked of the pig, the duck, and the cat.

Pig: I will!

Narrator: Said the pig.

Duck: I will!

Narrator: Said the duck.

Cat: I will!

Narrator: Said the cat.

Hen: Oh, no you won't. I found the grain of wheat. I planted the wheat. I reaped the ripe grain. I took it to the mill. I baked the bread. I shall eat it myself!

Narrator: And she did.

The Three Billy Goats Gruff

Six Parts: Little Billy Goat Gruff, Middle Billy Goat Gruff, Big Billy Goat Gruff, Troll, Narrators 1 and 2

Narrator 1: Welcome to our show. Today we will perform *The Three Billy Goats Gruff.*

Narrator 2: Little Billy Goat Gruff was strolling through the fields when he saw a rickety, old bridge. On the other side of the bridge was a meadow with green, green grass and apple trees.

Little BGG: I'm the littlest billy goat. I have two big brothers. I want to go across this bridge to eat some green, green grass and apples so that I can be big like my two brothers.

Narrator 1: Little Billy Goat Gruff started across the bridge.

All: Trip, trap, trip, trap, trip, trap.

Narrator 2: Just as Little Billy Goat Gruff came to the middle of the bridge, an old troll popped up from underneath.

Troll: Who is that walking on my bridge?

Little BGG: It's only me, Little Billy Goat Gruff.

Troll: I'm a big, bad troll and you are on my bridge. I'm going to eat you for my breakfast.

Little BGG: I just want to eat some green, green grass and apples in the meadow. Please don't eat me. I'm just a little billy goat. Wait until my brother comes along. He is much bigger and tastier than I am.

Troll: Bigger? Tastier? Well, all right. I guess I will. Go ahead and cross the bridge.

Little BGG: Thank you very much, you ugly old troll.

Troll: What did you call me? Come back here!

Little BGG: Bye!

All: Trip, trap, trip, trap, trip, trap.

Narrator 1: Little Billy Goat Gruff ran across the bridge. He ate the green, green grass and apples. The troll went back under his bridge and went to sleep.

The Three Billy Goats Gruff *(cont.)*

Narrator 2: Before long Middle Billy Goat Gruff walked up to the rickety, old bridge. He too saw the meadow with the green, green grass and apple trees.

Middle BGG: I'm the middle billy goat. I have a big brother and a little brother. I want to go across this bridge to eat some green, green grass and apples so that I can be big like my brother.

Narrator 1: Middle Billy Goat Gruff started across the bridge.

All: [Louder, as Middle BGG is bigger] Trip, trap, trip, trap, trip, trap.

Narrator 2: Just as the Middle Billy Goat Gruff came to the middle of the bridge, an old troll popped up from under the bridge.

Troll: Who is that walking on my bridge?

Middle BGG: It is I, Middle Billy Goat Gruff.

Troll: I'm a big, bad troll and you are on my bridge. I'm going to eat you for my lunch.

Middle BGG: I just want to eat some green, green grass and apples in the meadow. Please don't eat me. I'm just a middle-size billy goat. Wait until my brother comes along. He is much bigger and much much tastier than I am.

Troll: Bigger? Tastier? All right, I guess I will. Go ahead and cross the bridge.

Middle BGG: Thank you very much, you great big, ugly troll.

Troll: What did you call me? Come back here!

Middle BGG: Oh, nothing. Bye!

All: Trip, trap, trip, trap, trip, trap.

Narrator 1: Middle Billy Goat Gruff ran across the bridge. He ate the green, green grass and apples. The troll went back under his bridge and once again fell fast sleep.

Narrator 2: After a while, Big Billy Goat Gruff saw the rickety, old bridge. On the other side of the bridge was a meadow with green, green grass and apple trees.

The Three Billy Goats Gruff *(cont.)*

Big BGG: I'm the biggest billy goat. I have two brothers. I want to go across this bridge to eat some green, green grass and apples just as they did.

Narrator 1: So Big Billy Goat Gruff started across the bridge.

All: [Even louder this time] Trip, trap, trip, trap, trip, trap.

Narrator 2: Just as Big Billy Goat Gruff got to the middle of the bridge, an old troll popped up from under the bridge.

Troll: Who is that walking on my bridge?

Big BGG: It is I, Big Billy Goat Gruff.

Troll: I'm a big, bad troll and you are on my bridge. I'm going to eat you for my supper.

Big BGG: Really. [SMILES AT AUDIENCE] Well, come right on up here and have a feast then. [AGAIN GRINS AT AUDIENCE]

Narrator 1: The troll climbed onto the bridge. Big Billy Goat Gruff lowered his head and charged the troll! Big Billy Goat Gruff knocked the troll clean off the bridge and into the icy cold water!

Troll: Glug Glug Glug.

Big BGG: Brothers, that ugly old bully won't bother us again. I butted him with my horns and knocked him off the bridge and into the icy cold water. I've done my job and from now on we can come and go in peace. Now, I'm going to go and eat some of that green, green grass and some apples.

All: Trip, trap, trip, trap, trip, trap.

Narrator 2: Big Billy Goat Gruff crossed the bridge and joined his brothers. He ate the green, green grass and apples.

All Three Billy Goats: Munch, Munch, Munch.

Narrator 1: And that mean, ugly, old troll? He never came back to the bridge. He learned that being mean never pays.

All: The End!

Index